That's My Nanny Tee

A children's book to ease the transition
from parent to caregiver

TYRA SIMPKINS

PAGE PUBLISHING
Conneaut Lake, PA

First originally published by Page Publishing 2021

ISBN 978-1-64701-260-1 (pbk)
ISBN 978-1-66248-122-2 (hc)
ISBN 978-1-64701-261-8 (digital)

Printed in the United States of America

To my husband, my rock. Thank you for rolling with me.
To my mommy, for the stick-to-itiveness gene
and my dad for the gift of words that flow.
To all of my babies: my Booshe, my Noodle, and all those whom
I helped raise, including the very first two, Fella and Tam-mooke.

Get ready for the next beginning!

Whose face is this smiling at me?
That does not look like Mommy.

A
B C

No, that's not Mommy.
That's Nanny Tee.

Who is singing that silly song to me?
That does not sound like Daddy.

No, that's not Daddy.
That's Nanny Tee.

Who is reading my favorite book to me?
That does not sound like Grandma.

No, that's not Grandma.
That's Nanny Tee.

My Nanny Tee
is funny, kind,
and sweet.

13

My Nanny Tee makes
yummy food to eat.

14

My Nanny Tee hugs
and plays with me.

My Nanny Tee teaches
me to be me.

My Nanny Tee cares for me just for a while
And when the day is done—

She is gone with a smile.

About the Author

In February 2002, Tyra Simpkins was diagnosed with multiple sclerosis (MS). This married mother of two was faced with a challenging dilemma—what will her new normal life be? She started MS YANA (Multiple Sclerosis: You Are Not Alone), a nonprofit organization which provides advocacy, education, and resources for African Americans and young adults living with this illness. This was her main focus for over a decade. Being able to empower and help tens of thousands of individuals, their families, and various communities in the Maryland, DC, and Virginia areas should have been fulfilling enough, but the desire to create something new, unrelated to MS, was stronger than ever.

Introducing Nanny Tee

A business opportunity opened the door to Tyra's latest endeavor. People never say how expensive operating a nonprofit can be, and with two girls in college, finding employment offering flexibility and a livable wage was greatly needed. In 2015, Tyra Simpkins—wife, mother, daughter, sister, aunt, and nonprofit president—would take add two new titles: nanny and author! Twelve children later (including three families with multiples), Nanny Tee was a hit. Becoming a children's author was a natural progression to being a nanny. These little miracles can turn an everyday moment into a real-life teachable moment. And these moments often lead to really fun stories.

So thank you for your interest in Nanny Tee. May you feel joy and newness (as the author intended), pass that feeling along to the next person you meet, and never stop reinventing yourself.